797,885 Books
are available to read at

www.ForgottenBooks.com

Forgotten Books' App
Available for mobile, tablet & eReader

ISBN 978-1-333-54862-9
PIBN 10518358

This book is a reproduction of an important historical work. Forgotten Books uses state-of-the-art technology to digitally reconstruct the work, preserving the original format whilst repairing imperfections present in the aged copy. In rare cases, an imperfection in the original, such as a blemish or missing page, may be replicated in our edition. We do, however, repair the vast majority of imperfections successfully; any imperfections that remain are intentionally left to preserve the state of such historical works.

Forgotten Books is a registered trademark of FB &c Ltd.
Copyright © 2015 FB &c Ltd.
FB &c Ltd, Dalton House, 60 Windsor Avenue, London, SW19 2RR.
Company number 08720141. Registered in England and Wales.

For support please visit www.forgottenbooks.com

1 MONTH OF
FREE
READING

at
www.ForgottenBooks.com

By purchasing this book you are eligible for one month membership to ForgottenBooks.com, giving you unlimited access to our entire collection of over 700,000 titles via our web site and mobile apps.

To claim your free month visit: www.forgottenbooks.com/free518358

* Offer is valid for 45 days from date of purchase. Terms and conditions apply.

English
Français
Deutsche
Italiano
Español
Português

www.forgottenbooks.com

Mythology Photography **Fiction** Fishing Christianity **Art** Cooking Essays Buddhism Freemasonry Medicine **Biology** Music **Ancient Egypt** Evolution Carpentry Physics Dance Geology **Mathematics** Fitness Shakespeare **Folklore** Yoga Marketing **Confidence** Immortality Biographies Poetry **Psychology** Witchcraft Electronics Chemistry History **Law** Accounting **Philosophy** Anthropology Alchemy Drama Quantum Mechanics Atheism Sexual Health **Ancient History** **Entrepreneurship** Languages Sport Paleontology Needlework Islam **Metaphysics** Investment Archaeology Parenting Statistics Criminology **Motivational**

HOW TO PAINT SIGNS
AND
SHO' CARDS

By
E. C. MATTHEWS

A COMPLETE COURSE OF SELF-INSTRUCTION CONTAINING 100 ALPHABETS AND DESIGNS

Copyright, 1920, by
J. S. Ogilvie Publishing Company

NEW YORK
J. S. Ogilvie Publishing Company
57 Rose Street

TT 360
M3

AUG -9 1920
© Cl. A 571945

CONTENTS

	PAGE
INTRODUCTION	3
ALPHABETS	6
COMPOSITION	13
COLOR COMBINATIONS	18
HOW TO MIX PAINTS	22
SHOW CARDS	29
WINDOW SIGNS	35
BANNERS	41
BOARD AND WALL SIGNS	45
READY MADE LETTERS	49
GILDING	52
COMMERCIAL ART	58
TRICKS OF THE TRADE	63

Introduction

THERE are many sign painters' books on the market to-day, but no one of them covers all practical work in a brief, understandable way.

That is just what this book is intended for.

Sign painting is an art, but anyone who can read and write may learn to paint passably good signs within a reasonable length of time by following the directions given herein.

A good sign painter is often referred to as a genius; genius is nine-tenths hard work.

Anyone who finds joy in creating and can stick to his work can be a genius.

The so-called "born artists" are no more born with the ability to paint than men are born with the ability to read and write, you must study and practice.

Some people learn more rapidly than others, but anyone can learn who wills to do it.

It was almost ten years ago when I made my first attempt at sign painting. I tried to get a boy's job in a regular shop but was unable to get on, so I started out to be a self-made painter.

I could not draw any one alphabet correctly and was one of the fools who drew letters out of his head.

Ye Gods what a headache I should have had! After a few months I grew discouraged and gave it up.

Then after a couple of years of other work the bug came back and I tried it again and stuck for almost three months.

HOW TO PAINT SIGNS AND SHO' CARDS

I am merely telling this in order that other beginners may avoid my mistakes.

The cause of both those failures was wrong materials, lack of lettering knowledge, and a touch of plain indolence. Even if I had worked harder I could not have overcome the handcap of wrong material and lack of information.

Then for two years I dropped sign painting and followed other work, but most of my spare time was spent studying drawing.

When I made my third attempt I was able to draw the Egyptian and Roman alphabets fairly well, and could draw pictures better than the average sign painter. Also I was fortunate in getting some personal instruction in the kinds of brushes and paints to use for different kinds of work.

My first attempts were very crude and my brush strokes were very crooked and ragged, but I was on the right track at last, and in less than one year (please excuse the egotism) I was able to paint better signs than some other men I have met who have been making a living and passing as sign painters for ten or twenty years.

Now I cannot give you the "sticktoitiveness" which you will need. That's up to you, but I shall be very careful to give you the right idea in regard to material, and methods of working.

Take this warning and don't try to paint signs with brushes and paints from the ten cent stores.

A long, limber camel's hair lettering pencil may seem clumsy when you attempt to paint on glass, but it is the proper tool and you will soon get used to using it.

I have met many self-made sign painters who were splendid artists and they invariably agreed

HOW TO PAINT SIGNS AND SHO' CARDS

with me that the worst mistake an amateur makes is in his selection of material.

Carefully study the lists of things you will need, mentioned in the following chapters, and you may save yourself many dollars and many discouraging failures.

There are hundreds of things on the market in the way of art materials which are absolutely worthless to the practical sign painter.

A good workman needs few tools and when a man has learned to keep his brushes perfectly clean, and to keep his material in good order, he has already made a good start toward learning the trade.

The methods described in this book are not intended to cover shop practice in the large shops, but are intended for the man who works in a smaller way.

There are several larger and more elaborate books on the market which are intended for the more professional workman, and as you progress with your work I advise you to buy and study all of them.

The author has been a "rolling stone" for some years past and he wishes to thank the sign painters whom he has met in his travels, and also the authors of many contemporary books, for things they have contributed to this book.

The beginner at sign painting, show card writing, or commercial art, should learn to draw a few standard alphabets perfectly before he tries to sell his work. You may use a blackboard and chalk, wrapping paper and charcoal sticks, or a tablet and lead pencil in learning to draw the alphabets.

Rule a line for the top and one for the bottom of your line of letters. Draw the letters carefully, giving close attention to every detail, be careful to keep the letters in proper proportion to each other, thus—the letter A is much wider than the letter L, etc.

I advise you to begin with the Egyptian alphabet and master this so that you can make any combination of words fit into any reasonable shape or size of space.

Be careful to make your letters perfectly perpendicular, make the straight lines perfectly straight, and make the curved parts curve perfectly in one unbroken curve.

Keep the body of the letters all of one width; be careful of this; if your letter I is heavier than the curved stroke of the round letters it immediately stands out as amateur work.

You will learn to judge and criticize your own work in a short time, which is better for you than to have others show you your mistakes.

MODERN EGYPTIAN. 4

ABCDEFGH
IJKLMNOP
RSTUVWX
YZ & & 1234
56789 abcd
efghijklmnop
qrstuvwxyz.

HOW TO PAINT SIGNS AND SHO' CARDS

Keep the space between letters well balanced, that is, make the amount of white space between letters about the same all the way through every line of lettering. Usually the white space appearing inside of the round letters O, D, etc., should be greater than the white space between letters. Avoid making the inside space and space between letters equal, as it will make the lettering look monotonous.

Round letters, such as C, O, G, etc., should be spaced closer together than square letters such as H and I.

The letters A and T may lap over each other a little, while M and N need to be set further apart; the idea is to keep an equal amount of white between letters rather than to keep the letters a certain distance apart. See Fig. 9.

The standard Egyptian capital letter is about four-fifths as wide as it is high. The letters E, F, J and L should not be quite so wide, while the letters A, M, V, W and Y are wider than the other letters. In some modified and modern alphabets the round letters O, C and G are made wider than any of the other letters. These sizes are only approximate, the experienced sign painter or lettering artist does not need to measure his letters or spaces with a rule, but gets more pleasing results by lettering free hand and leaving the spacing to the judgment of his eye.

In lettering any large amount of reading matter it is better to use the lower case or small Egyptian letters in preference to the capital or upper case letters, because they are easier to read. Our eyes are trained to read lower case letters a word at a time while the capitals are more likely to be spelled out or read a letter at a time.

ROMAN

ABCDEFI
GHJKLMN
OPQRSTU
VWXYZabc
defghijklmno
pqrstuvwxyz

HOW TO PAINT SIGNS AND SHO' CARDS

The beauty of the Egyptian alphabet is in the grace of the lower case letters, while the beauty of Roman lettering is best shown in the capitals.

The Egyptian letter being very plain can be modified and stretched into many different shapes without becoming illegible. This and the fact that it can be made more rapidly than the spurred letters has made it a favorite style among sign painters and commercial artists.

When you have fully mastered the Egyptian alphabet, the Roman should be your next study.

The shapes are practically the same only the Roman is a thick and thin letter and has spurs at the points.

The Roman capital letters were brought to a state of perfection about two thousand years ago, and have not been improved upon since.

The lower case letters were not introduced until some centuries later, and were brought to their present standard shape by the Italians in the fifteenth century.

In drawing the Roman letters make all the heavy lines of one width throughout the line of lettering and all the light lines must be of one width.

Be especially careful to put the heavy stroke of all letters in the proper place. Don't put the heavy stroke of the A and V on the same side of the letter. Remember this rule for thick and thin letters.—

All lines which slant down and to the left are light and all lines which slant down and to the right are heavy. See Fig. 8.

The letter Z is the only possible exception to this rule, it is drawn with the slanting line either light or heavy, according to the alphabet you are using.

LIGHT SCRIPT - 16

ABCDEF
GHIJKL
MNOPQR
STUVW
XYZ& abc
-E.L.M.-
-1920-
defghijklmno
pqrstuvwxyz

HOW TO PAINT SIGNS AND SHO' CARDS

Sharp pointed and rounded letters should be slightly higher than the others. The points of the Roman A and V should extend slightly through the guide lines you have ruled on your paper. Also the O, C, G, Q and S should extend a little through the line. These letters should be only slightly larger and the difference will not be apparent. If these letters were kept inside of the guide lines they would look smaller than the square letters.

The Roman letters can be modified to suit special occasions with very pleasing effects, but don't attempt modifications until you can draw the standard forms perfectly without the alphabet plate before you to copy from.

The Roman alphabet is suitable for practically all work, and if you are ever in doubt as to what alphabet is most appropriate for your purpose use the Roman.

After mastering the two alphabets just described, the next standard letter is the Script.

In copying the Script alphabet make your letters quite large at first as you can see your mistakes easier in that way.

Try always to make your script lettering look like one continuous flow of harmonious curves; make every curve smooth and graceful without sudden breaks or clumsy shapes.

The Script alphabet is easier to draw and usually looks better when set at a slant, and you should be careful to keep your letters at the same slant throughout the composition,—usually 30 or 35 degrees.

If you are using a drawing board and T square you can buy a 30 x 60 degree triangle at any art

OLD ENGLISH

A B C D E
F G H I J K
L M N O P
Q R S T U
V W X Y Z

abcdefghi
jklmnopqr
stuvwxyz

HOW TO PAINT SIGNS AND SHO' CARDS

store and it will be a great help in making slant letters.

The light Script is a dainty letter and may be used to the best advantage on signs of a dainty character such as for millinery or candy stores.

Old English is a beautiful alphabet but is little used because it is hard to read. And it should only be used where it is especially appropriate.

The four alphabets just described are the base of all other alphabets now used, and if you master them you have practically mastered all existing English alphabets, and you should be able to originate styles of lettering for all classes of work.

The Italic letters are a sort of combination of Roman and Script forms, and are supposed to have been originated by Petrarch, an Italian poet of the fourteenth century. They were originally used as lower case letters only in combination with Roman capitals; they will also combine well with Script capitals.

Italics harmonize with Roman letters and may be used for the text matter where Roman letters are used for the display or headings.

Like the Script, the Italics should be used upper and lower case only, that is, never use a whole word or line of Italic capitals. Use a capital for the starting letter and use small (lower case) letters for the balance of the word or sentence.

This also applies to the Old English, Bradley Text or any extremely decorative letter.

The Italics should be drawn at a slant and the same slant should be maintained throughout the line or layout of letteriing.

The Bradley Text, and other text capitals, are modifications of the Old English.

The heavy plug letter is a cross between Roman

JAPANESE NOVELTY 14

ABCDEFG
HIJKLMN
OPQRSTU
VWXYZ&

HALF BLOCK - 15

ABCDEFG
HIJKLMN!
OPQRSTU
VWXYZ&.

HOW TO PAINT SIGNS AND SHO' CARDS

and Egyptian forms. It is very good wherever a heavy letter is wanted and looks best when stretched out quite wide.

The Spur Egyptian (Fig. 34) is a modification of the plain Egyptian, and when once you have mastered the standard alphabets you will need no instruction on the others.

The Cartoon Poster alphabet is good for humorous story headings, etc.

The Japanese Novelty alphabet is good for Chop Suey signs, or in hand lettered headings for Chinese and Japanese stories.

The Tuscan and Round full block letters are good for heavy display lines. They can be formed as single stroke letters and may be spread very wide and modified in many pleasing ways.

The Novelty letters shown on the page of modifications (Figs. 34 to 41) are suggestions to give you an idea of forms you can originate for special occasions.

The half block letters are used mostly for "Cut in" work, that is, where you paint around the letters, leaving the wording in white.

The standard proportion is to make the letters about four-fifths as wide as they are tall.

The letters A, M and Y should just fill the square, the W is still wider, and the letters G and V are slightly wider than the standard four-fifths.

The letters F, J and L should not be so wide. The width of the letter faces should be the same as the letter I, which is about one-fifth as wide as it is tall.

You should draw this alphabet carefully and memorize the proportions of the letters; it will help you with all the other alphabets, as they don't vary much from these rules.

BRUSH STROKES FOR PRACTICE

Close Shade. Cast Shadow. 7 Split Shade. Relief Shades

HIJEFIEEE

Relief Shade. Falling Shadow. Wrong Side. Too Close. O.K.

THICK AND THIN LETTERS

MANY·MANY

WRONG   8   CORRECT

9   SPACING LETTERS

HIAT LAW   HIAT LAW

WRONG WAY   RIGHT WAY.

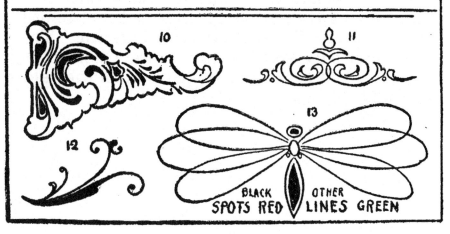

BLACK SPOTS RED   OTHER LINES GREEN

HOW TO PAINT SIGNS AND SHO' CARDS

You should know what correct proportions are, so measure your letters at first until your eyes become trained to judge correctly.

To the average person the art of hand lettering looks like a dry study, and they regard the work as a mechanical accomplishment. Nothing could be further from the truth. When once you have mastered the theory and practice of lettering, it becomes an art and is no longer mechanical. You can express just as much originality and personality in lettering as you can in pictorial work. The human figure has a skeleton and the artist must observe certain rules and proportions, else his work will look like a monstrosity instead of a thing of beauty.

So it is with the lettering artist; but when once he has the fundamentals of lettering he will find it possible to make hundreds of pleasing modifications; in fact, he adopts letter forms to suit every purpose and occasion, and his possibilities are as unlimited as in any art.

The Chapter headings in this book are examples of modified lettering. It is usually customary to keep such headings in harmony with each other; however, I have purposely neglected that in order to show many different styles of lettering. These were hurriedly sketched and are not perfect, but will give you some idea of the possibilities along this line.

COMPOSITION

Composition is as important in sign work as it is in landscape painting.

Good lettering doesn't make a good sign unless the layout or arrangement of the lettering is good.

A good composition usually contains an element of squareness, curvature and radiation.

The straight and curved forms of the letters may give the squareness and curvature while a bit of scroll work or a line of lettering arranged in a semicircle may add the touch of radiation to your layout.

Mechanical perfection in composition is not pleasing. A perfectly square sign is not as pleasing to the eye as an oblong.

A perfect circle is not as beautiful as an oval form or a circle broken by other lines.

The principal line of lettering should not come exactly in the center of a sign, measuring up and down, but usually would look far better if placed well above the center.

Your design should show harmony in its relationship. Block letters are appropriate for a hardware store or an ice and coal sign, and a light Script or other dainty letter should be used on the window of a lace and fancywork store.

Don't use Heavy Plug letters on a milliner's sign and Old English on the smoke stack of an iron foundry.

HOW TO PAINT SIGNS AND SHO' CARDS

A good sign must contain contrast as well as harmony. There should be contrast in the size of lettering, and the color of the letter should contrast as much as possible with the background. Wherever possible use at least two different sizes of lettering. Bring out the line of most importance larger than the remainder of the lettering.

Don't use too many styles of lettering on one sign, one or two styles is usually enough. And these different styles should harmonize. Roman harmonizes with Italic or Egyptian, but Full Block doesn't harmonize with light Script.

Full Block letters are very appropriate for a bank sign, because they look substantial. Where they are used for the display line Egyptian or Half Block is good for the small lettering.

When Round Full Block or Heavy Plug letters are used for display liues, plain Egyptian is good for the less important wording.

Roman letters harmonize with the straight lines of architecture, while Italics harmonize best with Scroll designs.

Now and then a line of lettering on the slant will kill the monotony of a "layout," but don't overdo it.

Try to keep your designs well balanced, don't crowd your words or make your letters too large for the space. A well-arranged layout of small lettering is easier to read than a crowded sign of large lettering.

Underlining a line or two of lettering will sometimes improve a sign, and it helps to "tie" the design together.

A touch of scroll work or a fancy initial will often improve a sign fifty per cent, but don't

POINTS TO OBSERVE.

KEEP SPURS SAME SIZE.

THE. 18 | 𝓃 19

SMALL SCRIPT LETTERS JOIN EACH OTHER AT CENTER

WHEN IT IS NECESSARY TO COVER PART OF A LINE OF LETTERS COVER THE BOTTOM AS THE TOP IS EASIEST TO READ

20 21 **HOT.**

Use square periods and commas with Square letters — Half Block & Full Block And round periods with round letters — Roman, Script, etc.

A period should be as thick as the letters it is used with.

DON'T CARRY HEAVY STROKE TOO LOW IN SCRIPT.

at — wrong. 22   right → at   Keep inside line almost straight

23 S S S

THE HARDEST LETTER TO DRAW — STUDY AND PRACTICE THES

5¢   Show Card Writers use 24 the Figure five a lot Practice it also.   5¢

carry the decorative idea too far. Scrolls and other decorations should be in a subdued color or they may stand out stronger than the lettering and spoil the sign. A plain neat sign is better than one which is over-decorated.

"Distance lends enchantment" in sign composition as well as in life. By using a shade under the letter or some other touch of perspective you can suggest the distance.

The shade should fall downward and to the left and usually should be set entirely away from the letter and not connected to it. See Fig. 7.

The reason for shading letters to the left is that it takes less time, as fewer brush strokes are required than for a right-hand shade.

A highlight will often improve the appearance of a letter also.

The highlight should be on the face of the letter and at the upper right-hand edge directly opposite the shade.

Where both highlight and shade are used the highlight should usually be lighter than the face of the letter, while the shade should be darker.

Display letters should usually be improved by outlining; for instance, if you were to paint a black letter on a green wall a line of white around the letter would be a great improvement.

An outline of blue, red or green is often used on aluminum window signs.

Face decoration is another method of improving plain letters. For painting face decorations use a color which contrasts with the background more than the letter itself does.

White paint is the best material for face decoration or highlights on an aluminum window sign.

HOW TO PAINT SIGNS AND SHO' CARDS

In making a gold window sign with face decoration, two colors of gold leaf are usually used. The outline and face decoration is laid with deep gold, then backed up and the surplus gold removed before the body color of lemon gold is laid.

If you paint plain black letters on a white background, a drop shade of light gray will greatly improve the appearance of the letters.

Letters possess character, and as the portrait painter strives to bring out the character of his model, so the sign painter should try to bring out the peculiar characteristics of the letter which he uses.

The plain Egyptian, Bradley Text and light Script letters are tall and may be made taller than standard proportions and still give a very pleasing effect.

If you want to make a living from sign painting within a short time, I advise you to give your entire attention to the Roman and Egyptian alphabets, and learn to make one good single stroke alphabet, say the Modern Text. The heavy Bulletin Roman is good for all-around work.

Stick to the three above alphabets and let the others alone for the first year or so; you can handle all classes of work and your lettering will develop character, while if you try to use all the different alphabets you will only confuse yourself, and will be unable to do anything well.

One of the best sign painters I have ever met used three alphabets exclusively on nine-tenths of his work. He used the plain Egyptian, Heavy Plug, and single stroke Italic. He was an unusually fast workman and his signs always looked snappy and full of character.

I have also known several fairly good painters

MODIFICATIONS

FIRE SALE

WINTER

RUSTIC

FURS

P. B. HEFK SR.

FULL - BLOCK.

MODERN.

HOW TO PAINT SIGNS AND SHO' CARDS

who used only two alphabets, usually Egyptian and Script. It is far better to do two alphabets well than twenty in a slipshod manner. Whatever alphabets you may select, strive to draw perfect letters, make the straight lines straight, the curves smooth, and the spurs sharp, and keep the letters in proper proportion to each other.

Speed is a thing which will eventually come to a good workman, but work for perfection rather than speed until you can really do good work.

Here are a few suggestions for making modified alphabets.

Never mix alphabets, that is, don't use Roman and Egyptian, or Poster and Half Block letters in the same word.

When you use a letter with spurs (Spurs are shown in black in Fig. 18), all the letters of the word or line should be spurred.

Or if you use a top-heavy S, the other letters which will permit should be top-heavy. See Fig. 39.

These modified forms may be used and the remaining letters made just as they are in the alphabet, plate No. 4.

Notice the ends of the letters C and S in Fig. 34; they are straight up and down instead of at an angle, as in alphabet No. 4. Therefore the ends of G and J would be made the same way to follow out the modification.

Color Combinations

The three primary colors are Red, Blue and Yellow.

Purple, Green and Orange are the secondary colors.

Purple is made of red and blue.

Green is made of yellow and blue.

Orange is made of yellow and red.

Given the primary colors an artist can mix any other color for himself. However, most painters buy the colors they want to use and mix colors only in emergencies.

When two primary colors are combined the third primary will be the contrast for the mixed color. Thus, if you mix red and blue you get purple, and yellow will make the strongest contrast for purple. Red contrasts with green, and blue is a contrast for orange.

Another thing to remember in color composition is that yellow has the appearance of coming toward the observer. Red stands still; and blue recedes.

Different shades and tints of color may be made by adding black and white. By adding a small amount of black to blue you get an indigo color, or by adding a large amount of white you get a sky blue.

HOW TO PAINT SIGNS AND SHO' CARDS

Black is very strong and should be added to other colors very sparingly· or you will get them too dark.

Sign painters use colors which are already ground in oil or Japan and seldom mix dry colors.

Colors in oil or Japan are in a heavy paste form and are thinned as used.

For work on glass, the color is mixed with varnish. For muslin, the color is mixed with gasoline and varnish. For wood, with oil and turpentine, and for brick walls, the color is thinned with oil and gasoline.

Where colors dry too slow, Japan drier is added.

Sign painters use the strong pure colors for most work, while house painters use softer tints which are made by mixing colors with a large percentage of white lead.

Tint is the proper word to express very light colors, or colors mixed with a large amount of white.

Shades are dark colors made by adding black to other colors.

Hue means a particular tone of any color, such as orange-yellow, or purple-blue.

The following primaries are most used by sign painters:

Vermilion and Para reds are used because they are more brilliant, opaque and durable than most other reds. Para reds are not durable if mixed with white lead,—this is usually mentioned on the label.

When necessary to add white to such reds, zinc white should be used.

Prussian blue is the standard sign painter's blue; it is semi-transparent, but being a very

HOW TO PAINT SIGNS AND SHO' CARDS

strong color it can be mixed with white to make it opaque and still retain a very dark blue.

Chrome is the sign painter's yellow; it comes in three shades:

>No. 1 Chrome, or Lemon;
>No. 2, or medium Chrome; and
>No. 3, or Chrome Orange.

The following list may be referred to for mixing colors: The amount of each color required is not always given because that depends altogether on the tint, shade or hue desired. But usually you should use more of the light colors than the dark ones.

Use a larger portion of the first color mentioned where exact proportions are not given.

Brewster Greene—Green, black and a touch of yellow.
Brown—Yellow, red and black.
Buff—White and yellow.
Canary—White and No. 2 Chrome Yellow.
Chestnut—White and brown.
Chocolate—White, burnt umber and yellow. Or red, black and yellow.
Citron—3 parts red, 2 parts yellow, 1 part blue.
Coral Pink—White lead 10 parts, Vermilion 3 parts, Orange Chrome, 2 parts.
Cream—Add small quantity of yellow and drop of red to white.
Drab—White lead 9 parts, Ochre 1 part, a drop of lamp black.
Flesh—White with a small amount of red and a drop of yellow.
>For a sallow complexion add umber or olive green, very sparingly.

Gray—White and Black.

HOW TO PAINT SIGNS AND SHO' CARDS

Green—Yellow and blue.
Lavender—Add white to violet, or mix white, black and red.
Maroon—Red and black.
Neutral Gray—Yellow, blue and red. Add white for lighter tints.
Old Ivory—White lead tinted with a few drops of raw sienna.
Old Rose—Carmine, white and a drop of black.
Olive Green—White, yellow, green and black.
Orange—Yellow and red.
Peacock Blue—3 parts white, 1 part light Chrome green, 1 part ultramarine blue, a drop of black.
Pea Green—White and green.
Pearl Gray—White lead and a very small quantity of red, blue and black in equal proportions.
Pink—White and red.
Pink Shell—White 50 parts, vermilion 2 parts, orange chrome 1 part, burnt sienna 1 part.
Purple—Red and blue.
Purple Lake—Vermilion and a little ultramarine blue.
Rose—Tint white with carmine.
Scarlet—Vermilion 8 parts, carmine 1 part, zinc white 1 part.
Sepia Color—Burnt sienna, small quantity of lamp black and Indian red.
Sky Blue—White tinted with blue.
Straw Color—White 8 parts, medium chrome 1 part.
Tan—White, burnt sienna, chrome yellow and raw umber.
Terra Cotta—White and a small quantity of burnt sienna, drop of black.

Violet—Blue and red.

Wine Color—Three parts carmine, 2 parts ultramarine blue.

How to Mix Paints

To break white lead properly for flat work you should stir in a small amount of turpentine and let it stand over night. In the morning pour off the milky liquid and stir in fresh turpentine. Repeat the above operation until the liquid is absolutely clear after standing. Then mix with turpentine and rubbing varnish.

To make white paint of the white lead, add linseed oil in the proportion of 5 gallons to 100 pounds of white lead. A pint of Drier may also be added. Or in winter time use 4½ gallons of linseed oil, ½ gallon of turpentine and a pint of Japan drier to 100 pounds of white lead.

For Primer, or first coat on new buildings, most house painters use 6½ gallons of raw linseed oil and ½ gallon of turpentine to 100 pounds of white lead.

White lead should be purchased already ground in oil, but red lead should be purchased in the fine ground dry state, and mixed as used.

Red lead is used for prime coat on iron work or where the finishing coat is to be red.

Red lead is considered much better than white lead for painting iron, or for boats and other surfaces submerged in water.

Gasoline is used for thinning white lead for brick wall or bulletin signs. Bulletins are not usually expected to last over six months.

But for house painting gasoline should never be

HOW TO PAINT SIGNS AND SHO' CARDS

used, and turpentine should be used sparingly on exterior work, or the paint will become chalky and rub off.

Paint peeling is usually caused by applying the paint too thick; by painting a second coat before the first coat is dry, or by painting on damp wood.

Colored paints are made by grinding the dry color in linseed oil and then thinning with oil and turps. Usually white lead is added to make the paint cover better.

(In mixing blacks and greens more driers are necessary than with most other colors. One of my first mistakes in sign painting was to mix lamp black with raw linseed oil. That was ten years ago, and I doubt if the black is dry yet. It wasn't the last time I saw it.)

To give you an idea of how much white lead is used in colored paints I am giving you the proper proportions of ingredients for a chocolate brown paint:

One hundred pounds white lead, 25 pounds of burnt umber, 10 pounds of burnt sienna, 4 pounds Chrome yellow, 5½ gallons of linseed oil, ½ gallon of turpentine, 1 pint of Japan drier.

This would make over ten gallons of very good paint, much better than any ready mixed house paint.

White lead is added to most other colors in about the above proportions, unless a very brilliant color is wanted, then less white is used.

For interior or flat coat work the paint is thinned with turpentine and very little oil is used.

Some pigments require a great deal more oil than others when grinding to paste form; for instance, 25 pounds of white lead will only absorb about 3 pounds of oil in grinding, while 25 pounds

HOW TO PAINT SIGNS AND SHO' CARDS

of burnt sienna would require almost 45 pounds of oil.

The following table gives approximately the amount of oil required in grinding raw pigments to paste form:

25 lbs. chrome yellow	requires	5	lbs. oil.
25 lbs. vermilion	"	6	" "
25 lbs. chrome green	"	5	" "
25 lbs. yellow ochre	"	16	" "
25 lbs. ivory black	"	28	" "
25 lbs. cobalt blue	"	31	" "
25 lbs. raw sienna	"	35	" "
25 lbs. Florentine brown	"	37	" "

Other colors require somewhat similar proportions; for instance, light red, light ochre, and zinc white require just a little more oil respectively than vermilion, yellow ochre and white lead.

This table is given for painters who use large quantities of paint and should not confuse the amateur sign painter, who is seldom, if ever, required to grind his own colors.

White is not strong but has the good quality of being opaque (that is, not transparent), and is frequently mixed with other colors which are somewhat transparent, such as Prussian blue, to make the color more opaque. Prussian blue, red and other dark colors are so strong that a small quantity of white doesn't materially change their appearance. But a very small quantity of color, such as might be in an uncleaned brush, would be sufficient to tint a whole can of white and spoil it for use as white paint.

Warm colors harmonize with each other. Red, yellow and orange are warm colors.

HOW TO PAINT SIGNS AND SHO' CARDS

Blue is a cold color and harmonizes best with other shales or tints of blue.

Black harmonizes with warm colors, and warm colors are used more than cold ones in sign painting.

To mix a warm gray to harmonize with other warm colors add a small amount of red and black to a larger quantity of white.

For a cold gray mix in blue instead of red.

Black and white make a very strong contrast and such signs are therefore easiest to read.

The eye sees white objects. If all the world were black we would be blind. When you read the newspaper you don't see the black lettering so much as you see the white blackground behind it, this enables you to read the paper; therefore, if the paper was black and the lettering white it would be easier to read.

I believe that white letters on a black background form the most readable sign that can be made.

Personally I think green and red are the best colors to use on an aluminum window sign, and they may both be used on the same sign for contrast.

Thus, if the lettering is shaded with red the scroll work should be green. Or if the display line is outlined with red the small lettering might be outlined in green, etc.

For transparencies I prefer black and white. A line of gold and red along the bottom will make the sign look richer.

For gold leaf shades and outlines, black is the old standby, but other colors are used a great deal. In New York, blue is used almost altogether with gold.

HOW TO PAINT SIGNS AND SHO' CARDS

Green and red are beautiful contrasts for gold, and small touches of these colors may be used to very good advantage in decorative work.

Black is the best color to use in combination with silver leaf.

Where red and blue are used on the same sign, they should not usually come in contact with each other, but should be separated by white. Notice how a barber pole is striped so that these colors are always separated by white.

When colors are used in making show cards you can usually get more pleasing results by using subdued or soft colors; that is, mix white with your colors instead of using them all as brilliant as they are when you buy them.

Bright colors are made more brilliant by surrounding them with subdued tints.

A sign must have contrast to be readable, don't try to letter on a dark background with a dark color. If the surface is dark the lettering should be white or a very light color; or if the background is white the lettering should be dark.

Red, Black, Blue and deep Green are the principal dark colors used. White, Chrome Yellow, Aluminum or Gold lettering shows up well on dark backgrounds and *vice versa*.

Where it is necessary to letter on a medium shade of Gray, Green, Brown or other background where neither light nor dark colors show up very well, you can get the necessary contrast by painting a dark letter with a white outline, or a white letter with a dark outline.

One thing which every amateur should avoid is the use of too many colors. Don't try to use all the colors you have on one sign. Simple color combinations are the best.

HOW TO PAINT SIGNS AND SHO' CARDS

It takes a man with a good knowledge of color and years of experience to combine many colors in one composition and get pleasing results.

Watch the good color combinations you see in show cards and other signs and try to adopt the best of them.

Following are a few good color combinations for signs and show cards.

The first four are harmonious combinations, and the last three are good examples of strong contrasts.

The contrasts are best, especially for most beginners' work.

Background	Lettering	Shade	Scroll	Border
Black	White	Dark gray	Dark gray	White
Light gray	Black	White	Dark gray	Dark gray
Red	Pink	Carmine	Carmine	Pink
Blue	Dark blue	Light blue	Dark blue	Light blue
Light green	Black	Red	Red	Brewster
Black	White	Red	Green	White or green
White	Red and black	Gray	Light green	Green or gray

In the last combination the large lettering would be red and the small lettering black.

Where white lettering is called for aluminum may be used if desired.

Experimenting with color combinations for practice is all right, but when you are painting signs for customers, use color combinations which you have already tried out and found satisfactory.

In different parts of the country I find many kinds of signs and different methods of working; for instance: In Washington, D. C., almost all the gold leaf window signs are one color leaf with a varnish outline under the leaf; while in St. Louis that kind of work is never seen. In New York

HOW TO PAINT SIGNS AND SHO' CARDS

most of the cheap window signs are tin foil on ready-made metallic letters. In fact, there is a greater quantity and variety of ready-made letters there than in all the other large cities combined. "Cut in" muslin signs are quite common, and transparency signs are painted in every imaginable color.

In St. Louis things are quite different "Cut in" muslin is almost unknown. Black and white is popular for window transparencies, and many of these have gold leaf outlines around the letters. Also some of the best shops in town frequently do aluminum window signs.

Chicago and Los Angeles are reputed to be the sign centers of the country; Chicago is there for quantity, but for class the Pacific coast is in the lead.

There is more of a tendency toward illustrated signs in some communities than in others. In Mexico most signs are illustrated, probably because there are so many people who cannot read. In most of our cities, illustrated window work is quite rare; but I have been called upon to paint pictures of almost everything imaginable, and a collection of good scrap pictures has proved very valuable.

Let simplicity be your guiding star in sign painting. There is a rich dignity about a good black and white sign which cannot be surpassed by anything but gold leaf.

Do not paint window lettering on the outside of the glass with dark red, blue or black as it will not show up unless it has a white background.

SHOW CARDS are classed as temporary signs and are made in an entirely different way from permanent signs.

Show card colors are ready mixed and are not waterproof. These colors come in glass jars and cost about twenty cents per jar. You can buy them from art stores or at most stationers.

Bissell's Velvet Black is exceptionally good. For most of the other colors I use Devoe brand; Carter's white and green are very good. These are the three principal makes; you can try them all and select the ones you like best.

If your color gets too thick thin it with water. A drop of glycerine added makes it work better. If the color has a tendency to rub off, mix a little mucilage with it.

Do not try to use writing ink, cake or tube colors, pointed brushes, or any cheap camel hair or bristle brushes for making show cards. Such materials mean wasted money and wasted time in trying to use them.

Show card brushes are round and made of Red Sable hair and are trimmed square at the end. Flat brushes may be used for very large work.

You should have about three round show card brushes to start, sizes 6, 9 and 12 make a good set.

HOW TO PAINT SIGNS AND SHO' CARDS

Dip the brush in the color and then work it out flat by pulling back and forth over a piece of glass or cardboard before you try to letter with it.

The brushes are round but you should always try to keep the hair worked out flat, and every time the brush is dipped in the color it should be worked flat before you start to letter with it.

Show cards are sold for a very moderate price and consequently must be made more rapidly than permanent signs.

Alphabets known as single stroke should be used almost exclusively. Single stroke doesn't mean that each letter is formed with a single brush stroke, but each letter is formed with the fewest possible srokes. For instance, the letter S can be made by the single stroke method with three strokes, while a finished Roman S would require a great many strokes.

The Modern Text, Bradley Text and single stroke Italics are all good alphabets for single stroke work and can be executed with either a brush or square point lettering pen.

The speed pen poster alphabet can be made quite rapidly as a single stroke letter by using a style B Speed Ball pen.

One line of finished lettering on a show card is enough, this of course should be the most important word or words on the card. The balance of the lettering should be single stroke. Many cards can be lettered altogether with single stroke letters, but learn to do them well.

Before you can master show card writing or any kind of brush lettering, you must learn to execute the practice strokes with a brush, see Fig. 6. When you can make these strokes free-hand in all sizes and positions, the lettering will be easy, that

SPEED PEN POSTER

ABCDE
FGHIJK
LMNOP
QRSTU
VWXYZ

HOW TO PAINT SIGNS AND SHO' CARDS

is, if you have already learned to draw the plain alphabets with a pencil.

Hold your brush lightly between the thumb and fingers, as you would a pen or pencil, or a little nearer perpendicular is better, roll the brush between your fingers as you make a curved line so as to keep it flat on the paper.

It is easier to work on a board or table which slants slightly than on a flat table.

Some card writers do all large work on an easel with the board standing almost straight up in front of them.

Always wash your brush carefully when you change from one color to another, as a drop of dark color will change the shade of a lighter color. Wash these brushes in cold water only. Also wash your brushes carefully before laying them away, if the color dries in the brush it may be spoiled.

Lay your brushes in a place where the hair will not be bent or warped out of shape. Red Sable brushes are expensive but with care they may last two or three years.

Most small show card lettering is done with a pen. I use a Sonnecken pen with an ink retainer or a Speed Ball pen for some purposes.

Use waterproof drawing ink in these pens, then clean them well after using and they will give perfect satisfaction.

For Script lettering use a small pointed Red Sable brush and outline the letters, then fill in.

A few years ago the shading pen was popular, but now very few card writers will use it. Also the air pencil and several other tools for freak lettering are not used by up-to-date card writers.

"Signs of the Times" is a magazine for sign

Bradley Text. ·52·

ABCDEFGH
IJKLMNOP
QRSTUVW
YZ & abcd
efghijklmno
pqrstuvwx
yz or dfgkl~
Style Week.

HOW TO PAINT SIGNS AND SHO' CARDS

painters; it sells for twenty-five cents per copy, or $2 per year. It is published at Cincinnati, Ohio. It carries "ads" of all the sign painters' supply houses. If you get catalogs from these houses you can learn a great deal about paints, brushes, etc., from them.

In making show cards the lettering should be laid out in a small space, leaving a wide margin all around.

For making the layout, use a piece of soft charcoal stick and the lines can be dusted off when the work is finished.

Some card writers use a very hard lead pencil and the light lines can be left on the card.

If you live in a large city study the styles of cards in the downtown store windows; you can learn more about styles of layout and color combinations by observing the work of others than could be put into a book.

An air brush is an instrument for spraying color and is used by many card writers for obtaining artistic effects. It is usually used with a stencil, that is, the part of the card not to be tinted is covered up with a pattern cut from cardboard or heavy paper. A complete air brush outfit costs from $25 up. You can imitate airbrush effects with a tin fixatif sprayer which can be purchased at an art store for about twenty cents. Or you can use a perfume atomizer. The color used for this purpose must be mixed very thin.

Dry color can be rubbed into a card with a piece of cotton, and many beautiful blended effects can be obtained.

For novelty effects a piece of wall paper can be cut out, pasted on the card and outlined as a panel, then you can letter on the wall paper with white or some other suitable color.

Seasonable cards, style cards, etc., should be decorated to suit the season. Following are a few suggestions:

Winter scenes for January.

Washington and Lincoln pictures, hatchets, cherries, etc., for February.

Easter lilies, rabbits, and scenes showing wind and rain or spring blossoms for March and April.

Flowers and flags for May.

Roses, brides and commencement scenes for June.

Flags and firecrackers for July.

Vacation scenes for July and August.

School scenes for September.

Autumn scenes with autumn leaves and colors for September and October.

Turkeys, pumpkins and corn shocks for November.

Holly, mistletoe, poinsetta, Santa Claus and snow scenes for December.

You can often cut suitable colored scenes from magazines and paste them on, then by outlining the edge of the panel with a light color the picture will appear to be painted right on the card. Diamond dust or flitter brocades make beautiful effects for some classes of show cards. You can buy it in packages for about twenty cents an ounce. An ounce will decorate a great many cards. To apply the flitter you should purchase a bottle of mucilage and a small camel hair brush (don't use your Red Sable brush for this). Paint on any form of decoration you prefer with the mucilage and sprinkle the flitter on while the mucilage is wet. After it has set and dried a few

HOW TO PAINT SIGNS AND SHO' CARDS

minutes you can shake off the loose flitter and put it back into the package.

Don't try to sell your work until you can do it well, then charge twenty-five cents and up for each card you make.

Show card board usually comes in sheets 22 x 28 inches and costs from four to eight dollars per hundred sheets. You can purchase it from a printer, or better still from a wholesale paper house.

Simple, full sheet cards bring from one dollar up. A Bill of Fare or other card containing a large amount of lettering should bring about twice as much.

Half sheet cards, 14 x 22 inches, sell for 50 cents and up; a card bearing an illustration should bring more than a plain lettered card. Charge for your time.

Quarter sheets, 11 x 14 inches, or smaller cards, sell for 25 cents and up, according to the amount of lettering. Air brushed cards are worth about fifty per cent more than plain cards.

Price tickets are worth from 30 cents to $3 per dozen, according to style, etc.

Single Stroke Italic - 53

ABCDEFG
HIJKLM^{c}
NOPQRST
UVWXYZ
abcdefghijk
lmnopqrstuv
wxyz - 12345¢
6789. For Speed.

Window Signs

Window work can be divided into four principal classes:

Painted or Bronzed Signs,
Transparency Signs,
Gold Leaf Work, and
Ready Made Letters.

In this chapter I shall describe the first two classes of work, the other two will be treated in later chapters.

Window signs are classed as permanent work and are painted with colors ground in oil or Japan.

Do not buy ready mixed paints for sign painting, but buy colors ground in oil or Japan. They come in one-pound cans and you can obtain them at any good paint store. The difference between oil and Japan colors is that Japan colors dry very rapidly; Japan colors are also called coach colors.

Colors ground in oil dry slowly, but they have more gloss and are more durable than Japan colors. Japan driers may be added to oil color to hasten drying. Linseed oil is added to slow the drying process.

To do aluminum bronze and transparency signs you should have the following materials:

1 lb. Vermilion in oil,
1 lb. Medium Chrome Green in oil,

BULLETIN ROMAN

ABCDEF
GHIJKLM
NOPQRST
UVWXYZ&

And
ONE CHANGE
By MATTHEWS

HOW TO PAINT SIGNS AND SHO' CARDS

1 lb. French (or Zinc) White in oil,
2 lbs. White Lead in oil,
1 lb. Coach Black (Japan Color),
1 oz. Aluminum Bronze Powder.

Several camel hair lettering brushes in quills, usually called lettering pencils, sizes 4, 6, 8 and 10, are convenient. They cost from 10 to 40 cents each.

One-half pint of Nonpareil Japan (this is manufactured by the Chicago Varnish Co.), other makes of quick gold size or coach Japan may be used, or, if you can't obtain this, a good grade of house painter's Japan will do.

One-half pint of Exterior Spar Varnish. A putty knife or paring knife, or both. Some turpentine, a chalk line, some chalk, yard stick and some old safety razor blades. The blades are used for cutting off old window signs and straightening out bad places in your lettering.

This selection of material will cost about five dollars. You should also have some kind of a box or carrying case for the outfit. Later you may add yellow and blue color, some linseed oil, a mahl stick, etc., to your outfit.

Now, if you have learned to draw the alphabets and make show cards you will have very little trouble in making a passable window sign. You will probably have some trouble in getting your colors and brushes to work right at first, but a little practice will overcome that.

First chalk your layout on the window, snapping the straight lines for top and bottom of each line of lettering with your chalk line. Then draw the letters lightly with chalk. This is done to be sure to get the spacing and balance right, and as you become more experienced you will not need to

HOW TO PAINT SIGNS AND SHO' CARDS

draw the letters in detail for this kind of work.

If your chalk doesn't mark well on the glass, hold it to your mouth and breathe on it, this will cause it to adhere better.

Be very careful to have the layout well balanced before you start to paint.

Aluminum is the most popular material for cheap window signs, it has an attractive appearance and will often last for years. Aluminum signs are painted on the outside of the window while transparency work is done on the inside.

Now to start your aluminum sign. Take an empty can or small cup and pour a small quantity of the Nonpareil Japan in it and add about one-half as much Spar Varnish as you have Japan and then mix in a small quantity of the zinc white, chrome yellow, or other light color, just enough to color it so that your brush strokes will show plainly on the glass.

(Different men have different ways of mixing "size," some use Japan only, others Varnish only, but I prefer a mixture.)

Now take your camel hair lettering pencil, No. 6 or 8 is a good size, dip it in the color and work it out flat on the side of the can, or on your putty knife, just as you work the show card brushes flat on the glass slab.

Now you can use your yard stick, or mahl stick, for a rest. Hold the lower end of the stick and the paint can in the left hand and rest the other end of the stick on the window. Now rest your right hand across the stick to steady it while you paint the letters. You can tie a small piece of chamois skin or cloth around the ball of the mahl stick to keep it from sliding.

If you have an opportunity to watch a good sign

HOW TO PAINT SIGNS AND SHO' CARDS

painter at work it will help you a great deal to observe how he uses the mahl stick and brush.

Try to keep your brush strokes straight and smooth and make the body of the letters all the same width. Amateurs usually have a tendency to make each succeeding letter a little lighter or a little heavier than the ones before.

If the sign is small you may be able to do all the lettering before you will need to rub on the aluminum.

You should empty the aluminum powder into a tin can with a tight lid and carry it that way.

Now take a piece of cotton cloth and fold it up to make a buff, then while the paint on the window is still tacky dip the cloth in the aluminum powder and rub it lightly over the lettering. (If you wait too long the powder won't stick good, and if you rub it on too soon you may smear the paint; after a few trials you will be able to tell when the size is just right.)

The aluminum will adhere to the size, and the yellow or other color will be entirely covered, the result will be a bright silver-colored sign which will never tarnish.

Some painters use gold bronze on the outside the same as aluminum, but I advise you not to do it. The bronze is merely fine ground brass and will soon tarnish or turn black when exposed, while aluminum, on the other hand, will remain white for years.

Now, when the aluminum is on, you may proceed to outline or shade the letters, whichever you prefer to do. Outlining is more difficult, so a beginner might use a shade instead.

Mix a small quantity of the color ground in oil, with Spar Varnish, and keep your brush worked

Heavy Script.

A B C D E

F G G J K L

M N N O P Q

R T U V W

X Y Z b h k

d g j l f q x z

o s u n m w.

out flat as before; if the paint is too stiff to work well you may add a few drops of linseed oil, turps, or Japan.

If you outline the letters use a small brush and keep the outline narrow; but if you shade them you may use a larger brush, No. 8 or 10, and make the shade quite wide. See Fig. 7 for shade explanation.

Red and green may both be used on an aluminum sign with pleasing results if you follow directions given in the chapter on color combinations.

The price of an aluminum window sign ranges from three dollars for a small job to $10 for a large job.

Transparency signs are worth twice as much for the same amount of lettering.

When you are able to put on a good aluminum job you will have but little trouble in doing a transparency sign.

Transparency signs are usually made along the upper or lower edge of the window, and a solid background is painted around them.

Black and white are the easiest colors to apply, so I shall describe the procedure for painting a black background with white lettering. When you can do this properly other colors will give you no trouble.

First mark out the sign very carefully on the outside of the glass. The half block alphabet is easiest to handle here at first as the letters are made up entirely of straight lines. Use chalk or keremic crayon for making the layout.

Now mix some coach black with varnish and turpentine, keeping the color thick so it will be opaque (meaning solid, not transparent).

Modern Text. 58.

ABCDEF
GHIJKM.
LNOPQR!
STUVWX
YZ-&- abc
defghijklm
nopqrstuw
xyz- ¢ $ Sit..

HOW TO PAINT SIGNS AND SHO' CARDS

Now you are working on the inside of the glass and the lettering will appear backwards to you. Take a camel hair pencil as before, only you must paint around the letter instead of on it. Cut in all the letters and paint everything but the letters solid black to the line you have made on the window for the edge of the sign. If you use coach color it will only take a few hours for the black to dry thoroughly; but if you should use oil color it should be mixed with Japan dryer and you will have to wait till the following day for it to dry.

When the black is thoroughly dry mix some white lead with varnish and linseed oil and paint the back of the sign white, lettering and all. Use a large brush and paint only a small part at a time; then take a piece of folded cloth formed into a ball or buff and pounce it up and down on the fresh white paint, then paint another portion and pounce it. The paint must be stippled in this way immediately after it is brushed on and before it has time to set. This will give the paint a stipple finish and no brush marks will show.

The white letters will show up well from the outside and they will be transparent enough for the light to shine through.

If you wish to put a gold stripe along the edge of the sign this should be done first.

Mix a little gold bronze (striping bronze is best) with Nonpareil Japan and draw the stripe with a striping pencil, which has longer hair than a lettering pencil. Then rub more of the dry bronze on it, just as you rub aluminum on outside work. This is not as good as gold leaf but it will not tarnish on the inside of the glass.

There are some ready mixed, and ready to mix, gold compositions on the market, but I have never

HOW TO PAINT SIGNS AND SHO' CARDS

found them as satisfactory as dry striping bronze and Japan.

A transparency sign will last longer if it is varnished after the paint is dry.

One of the great accomplishments of sign painting is to pull your brush with a smooth, confident stroke, and get away from dabbling or hesitating work. Always wash lettering brushes in kerosene or gasoline before and after using, and keep them greased with lard or vaseline when not in use.

Some of the instructions given for show cards and window work will also apply to paper, muslin and oil cloth signs.

Oil colors can be used for banners, but Japan colors are better for the purpose.

In either case the colors should be mixed with varnish and benzine and kept fairly thin.

The paper or cloth should be tacked on the wall at the proper height to work conveniently and the guide lines can be snapped on with a chalk line and blue chalk, and the lettering laid out with a stick of soft charcoal.

Most men work freehand on this kind of work. You may use your left hand for a rest, but it is not customary to use a mahl stick.

Before you snap the lines on an oil cloth sign take a cloth saturated with gasoline or turpentine and rub the cloth all over to kill the oily glaze which would keep the paint from adhering properly.

HOW TO PAINT SIGNS AND SHO' CARDS

Oil cloth comes in 48 and 52 inch widths, and the signs sell from $2 to $3 per yard.

Sign painter's muslin costs about 25 cents per yard; it is 36 inches wide and comes in rolls of 60 to 100 yards, or you can purchase it in smaller quantities at department stores. You can put a small shelf on the wall at the proper height, and by putting a piece of gas pipe inside the roll of muslin you can unwind the cloth and use it as needed, and by marking off the wall in feet and yards you can save time in measuring the cloth.

Poster paper for sign purposes is like white wrapping paper and comes in widths from 30 to 48 inches wide.

Muslin signs are worth from $1.35 per yard on up. A mounted muslin sign is worth $2 a yard and up. Cut-in work and signs with pictures or a great deal of lettering are worth considerably more.

Frames for muslin and oil cloth signs are made of 2-inch strips of lumber laid flat and fastened together at the corners with strips of tin or light iron and blocks of wood.

Camel hair lettering pencils can be used on muslin, oil cloth or paper, but there is a special flat muslin brush on the market which is far superior for the purpose.

Absorene or other wall paper cleaner can be used when it is necessary to remove the charcoal and chalk lines from a sign.

When you desire to make a long curved line on a sign you can drive a tack at each end of the line, then tie a piece of string to the tacks and let it sag to make the proper curve. Now make a mark along the string with a stick of charcoal

HEAVY PLUG   60

ABCDEF
GHIJKL
MNOPQ
RSTUV
WXYZ&
123456
789abcd
efghijklmnop
qrstuvwxyz

HOW TO PAINT SIGNS AND SHO' CARDS

and you have it. (You can buy prepared charcoal sticks from paint houses and art stores.)

Smaller curves can be made by tacking down one end of the string and tying a piece of crayon at the proper place to make the curve when pulled around the circle with the tack as the center.

Here is a good color suggestion for plain muslin signs: Large lettering red with light green cast shadow, small lettering dark blue; scroll or border, if used, light green. The green should be very light in color, about one part green to six or more of white.

For painting on canvas awnings use a stiffer brush than on muslin. Use Japan color thinned with benzine and varnish and the color won't spread.

If it is necessary to paint canvas with oil color, stretch the cloth and wet it, thin the color with linseed oil and paint while the cloth is damp.

Varnish is a very important article to the sign painter, and it might be well to give a brief description of the different kinds which are used most.

The most perfect varnish known was a Chinese secret preparation, used by them for thousands of years; it was as transparent as glass and practically indestructable; unfortunately, even the Chinese have lost the formula and modern chemistry seems unable to find the secret.

It was customary not many generations ago for painters to mix their own varnish, but it is now more convenient to buy the prepared article. Varnishes are mostly made from vegetable gums with a base solvent of volatile oils (turpentine, etc.), alcohol, or a fixed oil base solvent.

There is an almost unlimited number of dif-

ROUND FULL BLOCK.

ABCDE
FGHMP
JKLNO
IQRSTU
VWXYZ

MODERN ROMAN NUMERALS

12345
67890

ferent varnishes, and usually each kind is especially suitable for certain purposes.

Following is a brief description of the best known and most useful varnishes for sign painters' use.

Outside Spar or other good Spar varnish is the best all-around article; it is quite durable and is used for varnishing over gold leaf or other inside window signs, or it may be mixed with colors for outside window work, and is used for practically all outside varnishing.

Quick Rubbing Varnish is also much used by sign painters; it is frequently mixed with colors because it works easier with a brush than Spar Varnish.

Copal is a high-grade varnish. The base solvent is mostly linseed oil, which makes it very durable. The light colored grades are best and most expensive in this and other gum varnishes. Some Copal dries brittle and should be mixed with a more elastic varnish.

Damar is a colorless, elastic varnish, very good for stipple center gold work, etc. It is quick drying but too soft for most purposes. Don't use it for furniture or exterior work.

Hard oil varnish is quick drying and is principally used for cheap interior woodwork. In emergencies it can be used for backing up gold or for other purposes where a quick drying varnish is required.

Floor varnish is very hard and durable and can be used same as Spar Varnish. Varnish should not be thinned as a usual thing, but if it becomes necessary you may warm the varnish and stir in turpentine. Let the varnish set for at least an hour and stir it several times before using.

HOW TO PAINT SIGNS AND SHO' CARDS

Varnishes and paints should be kept in tight cans and instead of using direct from the can pour out the desired quantity into another can and use it, thus keeping the original can closed and in good condition.

Shellac is a gum soluble in alcohol only. It is very quick drying, and is used for stopping suction before gilding on wood, for covering up red and other colors to prevent bleeding when repainting, and also for finishing some kinds of woodwork. It should be kept thin with alcohol.

Asphaltum is a varnish made of mineral gum. It is black and semi-transparent and dries very fast. It has many small uses for the sign painter, but its chief use is for painting iron. There are two grades, T and B. T is mixed with turpentine and B with benzine. T is the best grade.

Asphaltum should be thinned with turpentine or gasoline.

For glazing, where a very hard finish is necessary, a little quick rubbing varnish should be added.

Never mix it with oil as it won't dry.

THE painting of boards or brick walls is vastly different from sign work on glass, and entirely different brushes are used.

HOW TO PAINT SIGNS AND SHO' CARDS

Bristle and fitch brushes are usually used for walls, and colors are mixed with turps and linseed oil instead of varnish.

Before painting a wall be sure just what lettering is to be on the sign, and decide just what space each line is to fill, and just how the lettering is to be arranged to give the best effect.

Different men often make different layouts. The principal point is to make the part of the sign which is most important in large letters, and keep the sign well balanced.

By counting the bricks it is easy to decide just how wide to make your letters.

You can usually make your line of lettering follow along the brick courses, and save marking top and bottom lines.

Wall signs usually have cut-in lettering. The wall is first given a coat of white, then the letters are "spotted in" or painted roughly with white or other light color, then they are cut in with the dark color and the background is filled in.

Black and white are usually used on plain, small or cheap signs.

Use white lead ground in oil for the white, and lamp black ground in oil for the black.

For cheap work the first coat of white can be omitted and the letters spotted on the wall with white and cut in with black.

The average sign requires at least several times as much white as black paint, because the white doesn't cover as well. White lead comes in kegs of $12\frac{1}{2}$ pounds or more.

On cheap walls the paints are thinned with benzine instead of oil and turpentine.

Benzine and gasoline are often referred to by painters as "benny" or "gas;" they are used for

MOVIE TITLE ALPHABET.

ABCDEFG
HIJKLMN
OPQRSTU
VWXYZ&

abcdefghi
jklmnopqr
stuvwxyz

HOW TO PAINT SIGNS AND SHO' CARDS

the same purpose, and either one can be used. They are used as a cheaper substitute for turpentine—often referred to as "turps."

In painting a raw wall the first coat of white lead it is usually thinned with half boiled oil and half gas, and the second coat with gas only.

On repaint jobs don't use linseed oil but thin both coats with gasoline.

Plain work on brick walls is worth 10 cents per square foot and up, while colored pictorial work is worth two or three times as much.

Most painters refuse to paint any kind of a wall sign even from a ladder for less than five or ten dollars, no matter how small it may be.

"Falls" hanging from the top of the building are used for large or high wall signs, but the smaller signs near the ground may be painted from a ladder

Always use your white brushes for white only, as black cannot be removed from a brush so thoroughly that it won't discolor the white.

A bulletin painter doesn't dip his brush in the paint and drag it across the edge of the bucket, but taps the brush back and forth on the inside of the bucket to get rid of any overcharge of color.

Always keep your letters close enough together to avoid a scattered appearance, and leave enough margin or border around the outside of the sign to prevent a crowded appearance.

Never paint brick walls with color ground in Japan.

Sable, camel hair, badger, or ox hair brushes may be used for lettering on wood.

In painting raw boards, the first coat should be boiled linseed oil with a small amount of white lead added, second coat white lead thinned with

HOW TO PAINT SIGNS AND SHO' CARDS

turpentine and oil, and third coat of color thinned with turps only. This gives a good flat surface for lettering.

On repaint jobs the first coat may be omitted and other two coats given as prescribed above.

For a cheap board sign some painters mix varnish with the last coat of paint, then when the lettering is on and dry, rub the board with some furniture polish in a cloth and it will have a varnished appearance.

In lettering on a varnished surface if the paint won't adhere properly, rub the surface with a cloth dampened with turpentine or gasoline to kill the glaze.

In applying aluminum bronze to size on a painted or varnished surface, it is usually best to apply the powder with a soft brush instead of a cloth, otherwise the aluminum is likely to adhere to the background and make the sign look cloudy.

Or where the surface is very tacky, mix aluminum powder with zinc white ground in oil and rubbing varnish. Thin with turpentine if necessary and apply as a paint, instead of lettering with the Japan size and rubbing the aluminum on afterwards.

You can mix aluminum with bronzing liquid or Japan dryer and letter with it, but the paint described above will cover better.

Where board signs are to be varnished, they can be painted with Japan or coach color.

Good board signs should be given a coat of finishing or spar varnish.

Following is a description of the principal kinds of ready made sign letters.

Wood letters for fastening on boards or wire screen come in perhaps a dozen different sizes and in many different styles.

The face of the letter is usually gilded with gold leaf when used. You can get price lists on these letters from Spanger Bros., Newark, N. J.

The gold and silver colored ready made foil letters are used on glass only. They come in sizes from 2 to 12 inches high, but the smaller sizes, 6 inches or smaller are used almost exclusively.

The lines for the lettering should be chalked on the outside of the glass and the letters applied on the inside of the window.

They are applied with a mixture of kerosene or gasoline and varnish. Different men prefer different mixtures, some use 4 parts kerosene to 1 part Spar varnish; but I prefer 2 parts of gasoline to 1 part varnish.

Great care should be taken to squeeze out all the air bubbles from under the letters before they are dry.

These letters can be purchased from The Metallic Letter Co., 412 N. Clark St., Chicago, Ill., or the Detroit Sign Letter Co., Detroit, Mich. Most of the painters' supply houses in New York

HOW TO PAINT SIGNS AND SHO' CARDS

carry the letters in stock, but they don't do a mail order business.

Delcalcomanie letters are often used for making auto monograms, and many large companies furnish Delcalcomanie window signs to retail dealers; directions for applying are printed on the back of the sign. The monogram letters may be purchased from the Globe Delcalcomanie Co., Jersey City, N. J.; full directions accompany the letters.

The other two principal kinds of ready made letters are white enamel and gold glass window letters. These are made in many sizes, but the 2 to 6 inch letters are used most.

Practically all ready made letters come in upper case or capitals only.

Gold glass and enamel letters are applied on the outside of the window with a cement made of dry powdered white lead, white lead ground in oil, and Spar varnish.

Mix the cement well by kneading and keep it very thick and the letters won't slide down the window.

Arrange your letters on the floor or table and see how much space they will require, then make lines on the window and apply the cement around the edge on the back of the letters with a paring knife. Have a perpendicular chalk mark through the center of the window or the center of the sign.

Now begin applying the letters in their proper places, putting on the center letters first and working out both ways, keeping the space between letters well balanced.

Now when the letters are all on, wipe off the surplus cement and the chalk lines and the result will be an attractive and well balanced sign.

HOW TO PAINT SIGNS AND 'SHO' CARDS

Old letters can be removed from the window with a paring knife or a thin flexible putty knife.

Sometimes the cement gets so hard that it is almost impossible to take gold glass letters off without breaking them. In this case take a small bottle of sulphuric acid and a glass rod or fountain pen filler and place a few drops of the acid on top of the cement behind the letter; this will eat down through the cement and soften it.

Be very careful not to get the acid on yourself or your clothes as it will eat there also.

Do not try to use the acid on white enamel letters as it will act on the copper and the heat might crack the window.

Plain white enamel window signs sell for six cents an inch and up. Thus you would charge your customer 30 cents each, for 5 inch white enamel letters. This is the minimum price; many shops charge more, and prices on the letters are still advancing. Script enamel signs are made up to order and cost several times as much as the block letters.

Gold glass letters sell for twelve and one-half or fifteen cents an inch. Thus 6 inch letters sell for 75 to 90 cents each, or 2 inch letters 25 to 30 cents each.

You can get wholesale prices on enamel letters from the Manhattan Dial Mfg. Co., 38-42 Lexington Ave., Brooklyn, New York.

Gilding

Applying gold leaf to glass, wood or metal is known as gilding. It is the highest branch of the sign painter's art and should not be attempted until you have mastered the other branches.

But when you are able to do a good job on other kinds of window signs, gilding will prove easier than you probably expect.

Following is the list of materials you will need beside the list given under window signs.

Gold Leaf: This comes in books of 25 leaves, 3¼ inches square with sheets of tissue paper between the leaves. It costs about 75 cents per book.

The gold is much thinner than tissue and it would take thousands of leaves of the gold alone to make a pile one inch high. It is very delicate and cannot be handled with the fingers. Handle the books carefully and do not allow anything oily to touch the gold.

Next you will need a gilder's tip for handling the gold. These are thin camel hair brushes mounted in cardboard; they are about four inches wide and the hair is about two inches long.

Handle the tip carefully and keep it away from your paints. It costs about 35 cents.

A water size brush 1½ or 2 inches wide is made

HOW TO PAINT SIGNS AND SHO' CARDS

of soft camel hair in wood handle; costs about one dollar. Never use this brush in paint.

Now the remaining list of necessary material can be purchased at any drug store.

No. 0, or four grain, empty gelatin capsules, 10 cents.

Absorbent cotton, 10 cents.

Powdered whiting, 10 cents.

Some grain alcohol.

(Avoid the use of wood alcohol as it is likely to cause blindness.)

Most painters use an alcohol heater for boiling water size, or you can boil it on a stove.

Now this is the way to proceed on your first window job in gold.

Draw your entire design carefully on the outside of the window with chalk or Keremic crayon. For very small designs draw the layout on a piece of paper and make a pounce pattern of it.

Wash the inside of the window well with whiting and water, then when this is rubbed off go over the part where the sign is to be with a cloth saturated in alcohol, and polish the glass with tissue paper; now be very careful to keep the window clean and don't touch it with your fingers.

Next take a perfectly clean vessel and put in one pint of clean water—distilled water is best—then put in four No. 0 size gelatine capsules, or a piece of fish glue the size of a nickel coin, and put the can on stove to heat, allow water to come to a boil and boil for five minutes, then strain through clean cheese cloth.

Now apply this freely to the window with your **size** brush, beginning at the upper left hand corner (if you are right handed) of the layout and **size** only a part of the design at a time.

HOW TO PAINT SIGNS AND SHO' CARDS

Take a piece of stiff cardboard slightly larger than the book of gold and lay the book on top of it. Hold this in your left hand.

It is hard to lay whole leaves of gold, so fold the tissue paper cover back half way and cut the gold leaf in two with the nail of your little finger along the fold of the paper.

This is done with the right hand which also carries the gilding tip.

Now rub the gilding tip across the hair of your head and pick up the gold with it, then carry the gold to the wet window and as soon as the gold touches the size it will jump from the tip to the glass. Don't allow the tip to touch the glass.

Leaf the window solid where the design is to be. Keep the window wet ahead of your work, but don't allow the water size to flow over the gold which has just been laid or you will wash it off.

Allow the leaves of gold to lap about a quarter of an inch over each other. Don't be stingy with your gold but allow a margin around the space where the design is to be.

Now when the gold has dried good and bright, which may take less than an hour or maybe even longer, depending on the weather, etc., you should take a piece of soft absorbent cotton and brush off the loose gold, then burnish by rubbing the gold briskly but very lightly with a clean wad of cotton.

Now you will see many holes and imperfections in your gild, so give the whole design another coat of water size; don't brush it too much this time or you may rub off the gold.

Now apply small pieces of gold to the holes or "holidays" and allow the gold to dry again, then

HOW TO PAINT SIGNS AND SHO' CARDS

brush off loose gold and burnish as before. Sometimes even a third gild is necessary.

After the holes are patched and everything is dry go over the back of the gold with hot water or hot size; this is called washing and it gives the gold a high burnish.

Now when the gold is dry again, back up or paint the back of the letters with black in Japan and thinned with Nonpareil Japan, and a little turps if necessary.

You can use a yard stick and a hard lead pencil to cut the bottom and top lines of your lettering straight. Just lay the rule against the glass and scratch a light line in the gold.

When your back up color is dry take a piece of cotton and breathe on it to keep it slightly damp, then rub it on the window to clean off all the surplus gold which is not painted under.

When this is all cleaned, take a safety razor blade to straighten up any ragged places, then outline or shade your letters with black or other suittable color.

When this is dry the sign should be varnished with good Spar varnish, allowing the varnish to extend slightly beyond the plate all around the letters.

A few drops of fat oil, or even raw oil, added to your varnish will make it more elastic and less likely to crack and peel.

Gold leaf signs on windows are worth $2 per foot and up. That is, two dollars for each lineal foot of lettering under five inches high. Scrolls are measured also, and fractions of feet are counted as full feet. No matter how small the job may be, it is not worth while to **do a gold** window sign for less than six dollars.

HOW TO PAINT SIGNS AND SHO' CARDS

Silver leaf may be used the same as gold leaf, only your water size should contain about fifty per cent more gelatine and you must use a badger or ox hair tip instead of the camel hair.

Never use silver leaf on wood or exterior signs. It will turn black.

And don't attempt to lay aluminum leaf with water size. Aluminum leaf is intended for surface gilding or outside work.

You can make a nice effect in one color gold work by outlining the letters with Mastic varnish or gold size Japan mixed with a very little lemon yellow, then lay the leaf on top of this and back up same as ordinary one color gold.

Or to make a dead center effect go over the inside of the window with whiting and water; this will leave a thin film of white on the glass. The layout should be carefully drawn on the outside of the window with a red Keremic crayon; if you can't get that, ordinary chalk or black crayon will do.

Now take clear, quick gold size and paint a center in every letter, the strokes will show plainly in the white. When this is dry rub the whiting off of the window and lay the leaf as described for one color work.

This gives a very good two color or dead center effect; at present two-thirds of the gold work in New York is done in this way.

Some painters use yellow color mixed with Japan for backup; thus no pin holes in the gold will show. In painting the shade or outline, go over the letters again with the dark color.

Prussian blue mixed with varnish is used almost altogether for outline and gold shades in

HOW TO PAINT SIGNS AND SHO' CARDS

New York. It is semi-transparent and gives a rich, glazed effect.

To make a good opaque black for shades, mix half lamp black and half Japan drop black and thin with Nonpareil Japan.

Asphaltum can be used to back up gold for a quick job.

For colored gold jobs, first lay leaf as for ordinary job, then back up an outline around the letters and clean off the surplus gold. Then fill centers with mastic varnish tinted with desired transparent color. When dry gild with lemon gold leaf using water size and back up same as ordinary job.

When backup color dries too slow you can rub over it with bronze powder and save a lot of time.

For gilding on wood or metal or on the outside of windows, mix Nonpareil Japan with just a little yellow color and letter in the regular way; when this has dried until it has only a very slight tack, apply patent gold leaf, rubbing it on lightly through the tissue.

Patent gold is mounted on tissue paper for gilding in the wind.

After the sign is gilded burnish the letters lightly with a wad of cotton and outline with color.

Ordinary loose gold leaf can also be used for surface gilding, but it takes more practice to lay it properly.

In making large smalted gold signs the lettering should be marked out on the board and given a coat of shellac, to stop suction. Then the letters are sized with quick size or fat oil size.

Fat oil size is specially prepared from aged linseed oil and dries to gild in from 12 to 48 hours.

After the letters are sized and gilded they are

HOW TO PAINT SIGNS AND SHO' CARDS

cut in with lamp black in oil mixed with about one-third white lead and thinned with boiled linseed oil. Then lay the board flat and sprinkle the smalts on while the paint is wet. Smalt should be a quarter inch deep.

In throwing off surplus smalts do it with a quick toss of the board. If the board is tipped up and the smalts allowed to slide over the gold it will scratch it and spoil the appearance of the sign.

To paint auto monograms, first make a pounce pattern of the design, then rub a raw cut potato on the place to be lettered to prevent the gold from sticking to the varnish.

Now pounce the pattern on both sides of the car. Mix a small quantity of tube yellow with Nonpareil and paint the monograms. When the size gets well set with just a little tack, apply the gold leaf. Brush off loose gold and outline with color. Charge $3 and up for monograms.

LINE drawings are the principal form of Commercial Art work. They are cheaper to

HOW TO PAINT SIGNS AND SHO' CARDS

reproduce than any other kind of art work.

Such drawings must be made pure black and white with no gray tones or colors.

The different shades and tones are represented with combinations of black and white lines or dots.

Such drawings are made with pen and ink and are usually made a good deal larger than you see printed and are reduced by photography when the printing cut is made.

The original designs and alphabet plates for this book were mostly 2½ times as large as they are printed, for instance, the alphabet cuts are 3¼ x 5 inches face measurement, while the original drawings were 8⅛ x 12½ inches.

The chapter headings in this book are something like the ordinary run of pen and ink work; they were hastily drawn, but most commercial work must be dashed off on short notice.

If you should copy any of these for practice work make your drawings about three times as wide as the prints.

Now regarding materials. Here is exactly what you will need:

Drawing Paper:—There are many good makes; an ordinary linen tablet is good for pencil sketching. For pen work I prefer high finish two-ply Strathmore or Bainbridge Bristol Board.

Waterproof Black Drawing Ink:—Higgins' is considered the standard make.

Drawing Pens:—Here are the ones used by all the leading pen artists: Crow quill, Gillott's No. 170, 290, 303 or 404. Spencerian No. 5 or No. 12. Try them all and select the ones you like best. Gillott's 303 is used more than any one kind and I consider it best for general work. They sell for about 15 cents per dozen and can be used in an

ordinary pen holder. Gillott's 1068 is a rigid pen of the same size and price and is good for fine lettering.

You should also have a drawing board, T square, 30 x 60 degrees, and 45 degree triangle, several lead pencils, a dozen thumb tacks and a piece of art gum for erasing pencil lines.

A compass with pen and pencil points and a ruling pen will also be useful. The ruling pen is not filled by dipping in the ink but by dropping a drop of ink between the blades from the quill of the ink bottle stopper or from a common pen. The ruling pen is not used free hand but alongside a ruler or irregular curve for making smooth lines.

Chinese white is used with a small red sable brush for painting under mistakes or otherwise improving pen and ink drawings.

The jar white is most convenient; Devoe's permanent white, Holme's white and Semple's white are all good.

The above material can all be obtained at any art store, or you can order by mail from the Devoe and Raynolds Co., New York or Chicago, or F. Weber and Co., Philadelphia.

Lead pencil drawings do not reproduce well, but a drawing made on rough paper with a Keremic or black grease crayon will reproduce nicely as a line cut.

You can enlarge pictures by marking them off in one inch squares and then ruling two inch or other size squares on your drawing paper.

The Pantograph is an instrument for enlarging pictures also, but I strongly advise you not to waste time with such mechanical means of drawing. Practice will enable you to draw correct proportions free hand, but mechanical methods of copying will never help you to become an artist.

In former years drawings were marked for ½ reduction, 1/3 reduction, etc. But it is better to mark them to reduce to four inches face measurement or whatever the size may be. When drawings are used in newspapers they are usually marked to reduce to 1 Column, 2 Col's, or whatever number of columns they are to occupy.

All writing on face of drawings should be done with a blue pencil. Blue does not photograph and the writing will not show on the cut.

In making pen drawings for printing purposes make your lines heavy enough to show up well when reduced, they need not be extremely heavy, simply avoid scratchy hair lines and keep the lines far enough apart so they will not run together when reduced.

One of the most important things in pen rendering is to make the lines follow the form.

Your paper is perfectly flat but you can suggest distance and form by the proper handling of lines and treatment of light and shade effects.

In making a drawing always consider what direction the light is supposed to come from and arrange your highlights and shadows accordingly.

Many artists make the first pencil sketch on a thin piece of paper, then when it has been altered and rearranged until the entire design is satisfactory the artist rubs a blue pencil, or even a soft lead pencil, all over the back of the sketch, and then transfers the drawing to a clean cardboard by going over the lines with a hard pencil.

After you have finished inking in the pencil sketch and it is dry, erase all the lead pencil lines with a piece of art gum.

HOW TO PAINT SIGNS AND SHO' CARDS

The decorative figures shown are rearranged from half-tone drawings by Mucha.

This is very good practice to render photos or half-tone pictures in pen lines. Your first practice, however, should be straight pen and ink copies.

Pen drawings are sometimes made directly over a silver print photo with waterproof ink, and then the photo is faded out with chemicals.

In doing pen lettering for reproduction use the ruling pen as much as possible as it will help you in making smooth lines.

Moving picture titles are lettered on dark photographs or dark cardboard with white ink or show card color.

The artist must be careful to avoid fine hair lines or fine pointed spurs on his lettering as they will show up gray instead of white when the title is photographed and thrown on the screen.

Some artists are using a brush instead of a pen for line drawings. Small sizes of pointed Red Sable brushes are good, and some artists use Jap art brushes.

Don't try to sell your work until it is good enough to be really salable.

Don't do careless work; draw carefully, lovingly and with feeling, and remember that nothing is beautiful in art unless it has character.

Whatever you draw look for the character of the thing and try to make every line a harmonious part of that particular object. This applies to everything, from the letters of the alphabet to the most elaborate painting.

A good artist is never fully satisfied with his work but is always striving for something better.

Lettering is the most important branch of Com-

mercial Art and good lettering artists are always in demand.

If you live in a large city it will pay you to attend night art classes and study figure drawing.

Nude figures are little used in practical work, but if you can sketch a nude figure in any position and then put the clothes on it, it is more certain to look natural and well posed.

The human figure is the most graceful form imaginable, and when you can really draw it well, other things will be comparatively easy.

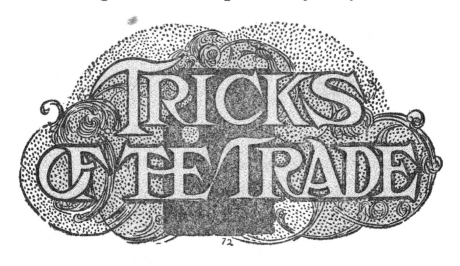

MAKE careful enlarged copies of the shoes and index hand, Figs. 46, 47 and 48, on fairly heavy paper, then go over all the lines with a tracing wheel, or punch holes along the lines about every sixth of an inch with a carpet tack. Then sandpaper the projections from the opposite side and you have a good pounce pattern for windows or boards. By turning the paper over you can make the hand point either to the left or to the right.

Select some suitable scrolls from the samples shown herein and make enlarged copies of them.

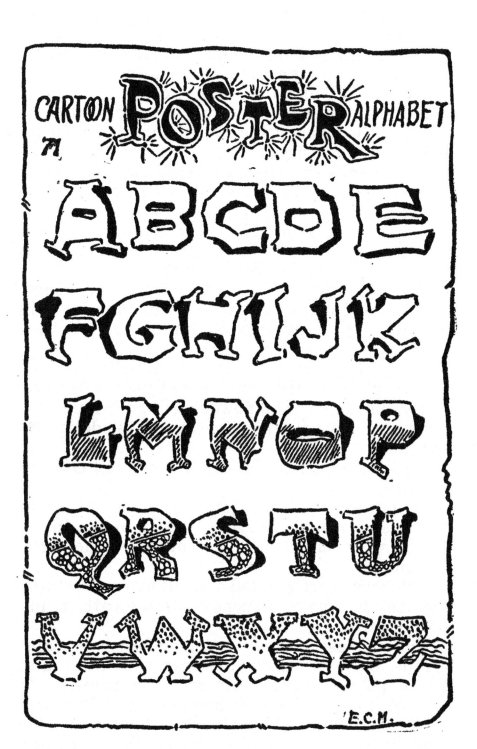

HOW TO PAINT SIGNS AND SHO' CARDS

In scrolls where the two ends are alike as Nos. 75, 77, 105, etc., you should make a careful drawing of half the scroll, then fold your paper in the middle, where the center of the scroll is to be, and trace the pattern through the paper, thus your design will balance exactly.

Such scrolls for window work should usually be about six times as large as they are in these prints. If the design measures 2½ inches wide your pattern should be about 15 inches wide.

When your drawing is complete, make a pounce pattern of it, as described above.

For windows take about an ounce of talcum powder, whiting, or powdered chalk and tie it in a small bag of cotton cloth, an empty Bull Durham tobacco bag is very good.

Now hold or fasten your paper pattern in the proper place on the window and pounce the bag of powder on it. The powder will go through the holes and leave a perfect outline of the design on the glass.

For white boards you can use dry red color in the pounce.

If your scroll is to be painted on the outside of the glass you can pounce the design on the inside if you wish and then rub it off after the scroll is painted.

After you have painted a scroll five or ten times you may be able to dispense with the pattern and do the scroll free hand.

You can use a small lettering brush to paint scrolls, but you can do it easier with No. 3 and No. 6 pointed camel hair scrolling pencils. If you can't obtain these at home, send to The Geo. E. Watson Co., 62 W. Lake St., Chicago, Ill., for a catalogue of painters' supplies. You can learn

HOW TO PAINT SIGNS AND SHO' CARDS

a great deal about materials and their uses from such a catalogue.

* * *

When you have an old board sign to repaint you can trace around the letters with an indelible pencil. Then paint the board with white lead and the pencil marks will "bleed through" so that you can easily repaint the old sign.

* * *

Kerosene is better than gas or turps for cleaning brushes or taking paint off of your hands.

Save all old muslin signs and send them to the laundry; they make the finest wiping cloths to be had, and it only costs a few cents a pound to have them washed.

* * *

"Taxtite," made by the Sherwin-Williams Co., is a paint remover which is unusually good for removing old window signs.

* * *

Turpentine flattens color or makes it dull; varnish mixed with color brightens it and preserves the brilliancy. Boiled oil dries quicker than raw linseed oil, and is therefore used more in sign painting.

* * *

Signs should be very briefly worded; four well selected words can often do the business better than forty.

* * *

For painting inside of windows plain black a mixture of two parts asphaltum to one part coach black is good, thin with turpentine when necessary. No varnish is required.

* * *

HOW TO PAINT SIGNS AND SHO' CARDS

Japan color is used for show cards which are exposed to the weather; letter with camel hair pencils.

* * *

To keep paint from peeling on galvanized iron, mix one pound each of Sal Ammoniac, Nitrate of Copper and Chloride of Copper in six gallons of water, when everything has dissolved add a pound of crude hydrochloric acid, then use a wide kalsomine brush and go over the iron with this preparation.

After twelve hours rub the iron clean with a piece of burlap and it is ready to paint.

* * *

Don't paint on the inside of a window when it is steaming or damp, even if you get the paint to stick it will soon turn white and peel off.

* * *

If you have trouble with an old color "bleeding through" when repainting a sign, put on a thin coat of shellac, which will dry almost instantly and stop the bleeding.

* * *

Gold leaf sometimes sticks to the leaves of the book in damp or cold weather; warm it before using. (Don't confuse this with patent gold which is made that way for gilding in the wind.)

* * *

The Tuscan Block letters, as shown in the word "Letters," Fig. 63, are drawn about the same as the round full block alphabet, Fig. 61, the only difference being in the formation of the block spurs.

* * *

Chrome yellow will show up some surfaces where no other color will.

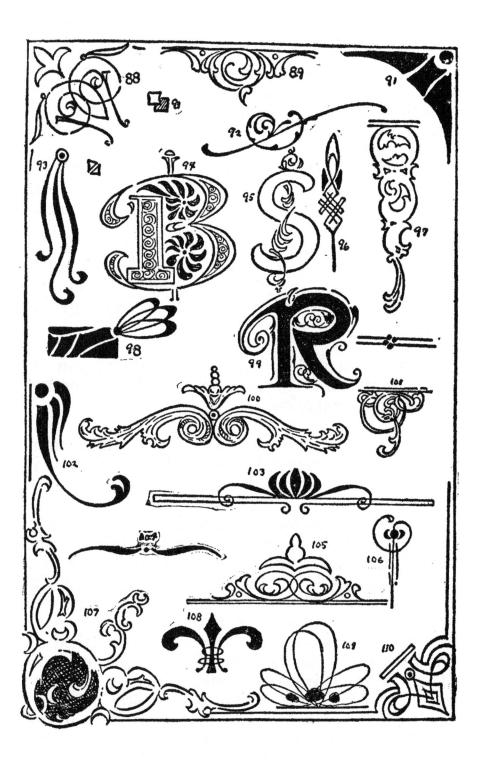

HOW TO PAINT SIGNS AND SHO' CARDS

Good material is less expensive in the end. A pound of good color ground in oil costs about twice as much as a pound of mixed paint, but it will paint four times as much surface and produce better work.

In buying camel hair lettering pencils be sure you get the best grade. They have long even hair cut perfectly square at the end and are firmly fastened in good quills with a piece of wire or a heavy indentation. You can fit wood handles in them to suit yourself. The regular sign painters' supply houses carry the good grade brushes, but many common paint stores sell a very inferior article.

Linseed oil will curdle Japan color if you attempt to mix them; they must be ground together to combine properly.

* * *

The Jewish sign shown in Fig. 49 is a meat market sign, sometimes the left half of the sign is used alone on restaurants, etc.

* * *

Large bulletins and brick wall signs are usually drawn to scale. That is, a small sketch is made of the proposed sign on a scale of about one inch to the foot. The sketch is drawn in perfect detail, showing styles of lettering, and picture well worked out. Also an explanation of the color scheme, or in some cases the sketch is worked up in full color. When this sketch has been approved, it is marked into one inch squares and the large sign is first given two coats of white lead and then marked into squares of one or two feet square to correspond with the sketch. This

HOW TO PAINT SIGNS AND SHO' CARDS

makes it easy to keep everything in exact proportion to the original sketch.

* * *

Mammoth muslin signs, theatrical backgrounds, etc., are usually painted in distemper color.

Distemper color can be prepared as follows:

Put one pound of Kalsominer's glue in one gallon of cold water and allow it to soak over night. Next morning put this preparation on the stove and bring it to a boil and add a few drops of carbolic acid and a tablespoonful of powdered alum, mix well and then gradually stir in dry color. Keep this on a low fire while using. Use fresco bristle brushes for detail or cutting in and large flat bristle brushes for "filling in."

Remember this paint must be used hot.

* * *

Printers' ink thinned with gasoline is good for paper or muslin signs, varnish can also be added if desired.

* * *

To prevent window sweating and frost on show windows in winter add two ounces of glycerine to one quart of 62 per cent grain alcohol and one drachm oil of amber; let stand until it clears and rub on inside of window.

* * *

When a varnish surface is too tacky to permit laying gold leaf or rubbing on aluminum bronze, you may overcome the trouble by mixing the white of an egg with two-thirds of a cupful of cider vinegar, give the surface two coats of this preparation and then you can do your lettering with quick size and apply the gold leaf or aluminum. It will stick to the surface but when dry the egg

HOW TO PAINT SIGNS AND SHO' CARDS

size can be washed off and you will have a clean job.

* * *

In painting a script sign first draw the top and bottom guide lines, then draw slanting lines across these every few inches to give the proper slant to the letters, now sketch out the lettering with a pencil or crayon, then outline the letters with a small brush and afterward fill them in. See Alphabet plate No. 16.

* * *

Never use your show card or distemper brushes in oil or japan colors. And don't put your oil color brushes in water.

* * *

To test dry vermillion, to detect adulteration, pour a small quantity of Muriatic Acid on some dry color; if adulterated the pigment will fade.

* * *

You can make your own academy boards for painting oil color pictures by giving any heavy cardboard a coat of shellac, and later a coat of flat light cream color, stipple with a wad of cloth while paint is wet. This gives the board a surface resembling canvas.

* * *

And now for a few parting words of advice to the amateur sign painter.

Read this book over several times, as you are almost certain to skip or misunderstand some important points during the first reading; also carefully study every illustration and make several carefully enlarged copies of the alphabets you intend to use.

Until very recently all sign painters' trade secrets were jealously guarded and a man had to

HOW TO PAINT SIGNS AND SHO' CARDS

work for many years to acquire even a fair knowledge of the art.

The secrets are no longer withheld and by referring to this book you can find the proper method of doing every kind of work now done by the trade.

With this much in your favor you should be able by observation and diligent practice to equal and even surpass the work of many old-timers within a very few years.

Keep your eyes open and observe all the different signs you see. Make notes of all the pleasing color combinations and notice how the professionals arrange the reading matter to make it attractive and legible.

You will soon learn to judge the different classes of work and even to tell one man's work from another. Apply all the knowledge thus gained to your own work.

THE END

Materials which you cannot obtain from your local paint store may be purchased by mail from the following dealers who specialize in sign painters' supplies:

WALLBRUN, KLING AND CO.,
 327 S. Clark St., Chicago, Ill.

GEO. E. WATSON CO.,
 62 W. Lake St., Chicago, Ill.

GEO. STEERE,
 434 S. Dearborn St., Chicago, Ill.

BERT L. DAILY,
 126 E. Third St., Dayton, O.

DETROIT SCHOOL OF LETTERING,
 Detroit, Mich.

N. GLANTZ,
 31 Spring St., New York City.

J. F. EBERHARD AND SON,
 298 Pearl St., New York City.

F. WEBER AND CO.,
 Philadelphia, Pa.

HOW TO PAINT SIGNS AND SHOW CARDS

By E. C. MATTHEWS

An up-to-date book containing a complete course of instruction. Illustrated with over 100 alphabets and designs, and written in plain English that everyone can understand and thus learn to paint good signs. Also suitable for commercial artists or anyone who has occasion to do hand lettering.

TABLE OF CONTENTS

1—**Introduction**; 2—**Alphabets**; Rules for drawing and spacing letters explained with simple diagrams. Contains fourteen hand lettered full page alphabet plates, including Modern Egyptian, Modern Roman, Bulletin Roman, Light Script, Heavy Script, Old English, Half Block, Round Full Block, Movie Title Alphabet, Heavy Plug, several "Single Stroke" Show Card Alphabets, and two Modern Poster Alphabets. Also many smaller examples, and rules for originating and modifying letters.

3—**Composition**; "Layouts" fully explained and illustrated.

4—**Color Combinations**; including chart.

5—**How to Mix Paints**; Full instructions regarding materials, quantities, qualities, and combinations.

6—**Show Cards**; What brushes, pens and other materials to buy and how to use them. Seasonable suggestions. Prices to charge, and some valuable "Stunts."

7—**Windows Signs**; A list of brushes, paints, and other material is given and the use of each explained. How to paint an aluminum, bronze, or transparency job.

8—**Banners**; How to paint paper, muslin, oilcloth and canvas signs. Varnishes and the composition and uses of each explained.

9—**Board and Wall Signs.**

10—**Ready Made Letters**; How to make a Cement for Gold, Glass, and Enamel Letters. To remove old letters without breaking, etc.

11—**Gilding**; Color Glazing, Dead Center, Smalted Signs, and making Auto Monograms.

12—**Commercial Art**; Pen and Ink Drawing for reproduction. Decorative female figures.

13—**Tricks of the Trade**; Useful and unusual "Short Cuts." The secret of Scrolling fully explained. Forty examples shown. Simple formula to keep show windows from steaming and freezing in winter. How to keep old color from "bleeding through." To make distemper color for Theatrical Curtains, etc.

This book contains 96 pages with 100 illustrations, including 23 full pages, is bound in cloth, with jacket printed in two colors. Sent postpaid to any address on receipt of **Price, $1.50**

J. S. OGILVIE PUBLISHING COMPANY

P. O. BOX 767, C. H STATION   57 ROSE ST., NEW YORK